A Guide to Historic Acushnet

A Peaceful Resting Place Near Water

By
Alec J. Plante

Foreword

For centuries prior to the Age of Exploration, the era beginning in the 15th century during which the most powerful nations on Earth competed to discover and conquer a "New World," a Native American tribe known as the Wampanoags lived in peace on the land today known as Acushnet. The town got its name from the Wampanoag word *Cushnea*, meaning "peaceful resting place near water." This book is a step-by-step guide to the most historic locations in Acushnet, organized chronologically by time of relevance. It was completed as an Eagle Scout service project, hence all proceeds will go towards the funding of the Acushnet Historical Society. Enjoy.

TABLE OF CONTENTS

- Howard's Neck and Peak Rock
- Samuel Sprague House
- Walter Spooner House
- Long Plain Meetinghouse
- Head of the River
- Acushnet-Wesley United Methodist Church
- Whelden Mill
- White's Cotton Factory
- Captain Franklyn Howland House
- Milestone 9
- Perry Hill Church
- Leonard Boat Shop
- Laura Keene Farmhouse
- Parting Ways Schoolhouse
- Long Plain Schoolhouse
- Russell Memorial Library
- Richard Davis Variety Store

HOWARD'S NECK & PEAK ROCK

Howard's Neck
First Settlement in Dartmouth (1660)

In 1660, John Howard, a lieutenant under Captain Myles Standish, was granted a ten-acre site on the Acushnet River, for the protection of subsequent settlers. The site was chosen because local Indians told Howard that its spring "never froze".

Four years later, in 1664, the three tiny settlements of Acushena, Ponagansett and Coaksett were declared the township of Dartmouth by the General Court at Plymouth.

Due west of this spot and presently uninhabited, the site is on private property.

Acushnet Historical Commission
November 1997

    The investors in Olde Dartmouth were growing restless. When 36 men were granted the lands along the Acushnet River by the Plymouth general court in 1652, they had no clue how long it would take before they would be able to turn it into profit. For eight years the Pilgrims sat and twiddled their thumbs, waiting for a fat-pocketed buyer to satiate their greatest desire: return on investment.

    It was a great deal, all things considered. The Olde Dartmouth territory had a strong river and acres of fertile land. Plus, there were no evil British tyrants telling you what you could or could not worship. The only catch: those darn-tootin' Indians. Native Americans frequented the Olde Dartmouth grounds in order to catch shellfish in the Sippican and fish at Apponagansett. This tragic flaw proved efficacious in turning away potential buyers. In response, the investors turned to Lieutenant John Howard, a valued aide to Captain Miles Standish himself.

His job was simple: establish a post within the Native territory where lands could be sold with guaranteed safety. Fortunately, Howard had allied himself with some of the local Natives years prior. Not only was he able to secure a post for the Pilgrim investors, but he was also able to set up shop along a stream the Natives claimed "never froze." From that settlement on what is today 89 South Main Street grew an entire town. It took four years, but in 1664 the Plymouth General Court declared the territory and its 56 new residents a township to be named Dartmouth. To separate themselves from their Native counterparts, the people of Dartmouth used a rock found lying alongside their settlement on South Main Street to draw a border between their civilized community and the Godforsaken Indian country. It was coined "Peak Rock," and upon this rock, Lieutenant John Howard built his church. This is where our story begins.

SAMUEL SPRAGUE HOUSE

Many of Acushnet's historic landmarks are often overlooked due to their unassuming nature. At first glance, such landmarks may just look like houses or rocks or trails. But once the surface is scratched, and what appeared to be minutiae is put in a historical context, that house you drive by everyday to and from work might turn out to be the oldest standing house in Acushnet. Such is the case with the home of the late Samuel Sprague, sitting pretty at 820 Main Street as pictured on the right. Sprague purchased the house in 1785.

Samuel Sprague, or "Squire Sprague" as he was to his business clients, was as active a member of the town of Acushnet as there ever was. He served as a representative of the town to general court, then became Justice of the Peace, then was elected into the Senate. He also dipped his toes into business operations. He operated dually as an advisor and lender for homeowners seeking help in managing their mortgages. But that's not all. Rumor has it Sprague is also responsible for founding the very first stagecoach route to Boston. Due to his ambitious career, Sprague was able to stash away a fortune and live his life in the comfort of financial security until the day he passed in 1825.

WALTER SPOONER HOUSE

Acushnet may seem like your run of The Mill (ha!) small town USA, but it and its residents have played an active role in the formation of this country. Walter Spooner, a revolutionary war patriot and a distinguished Acushnet townsman, may be the greatest testament to that statement. If you were breathing and conscious during the American Revolution and you lived in the Acushnet/Fairhaven area (considered the "Olde Dartmouth" township in that time), you knew who Walter Spooner was. Ladies wanted him. Guys wanted to be him. And the English feared him -- or they should have. Spooner served as the moderator for a conference that was to decide how the town of Acushnet would respond to the restrictions placed up on them by their oppressive English overlords. "Honorable Walter Spooner, esq." as he was known to locals, led the people of Acushnet against the tyranny of the British using his influence as a political leader. He served as town selectman of Olde Dartmouth from 1759 until 1772. The defining act of his career as selectman was approving construction for Acushnet's first honest schoolhouse, built at the Parting Ways crossing.

However, Spooner passed along the selectman gig when he was promoted to the Governor's Council. Governor John Hancock saw in Spooner a practical, level-headed leader -- just what the doctor ordered during the times of political instability that plagued the American Revolution. As a member of the Council, Spooner was able to sit in on the signing of the Massachusetts state constitution. This piece of legislature is still referenced in both congressional and judicial contexts today. Likewise, Spooner's homestead on Main Street is also still standing tall today.

LONG PLAIN MEETINGHOUSE

Acushnet is a town built on the shoulders of Quakers. When the Quakers were exiled from Plymouth and the Massachusetts Bay Colony in the late 17th century and labeled as "religious dissidents," they turned to colonies in Rhode Island. However, they eventually found their way back to Massachusetts and settled into the Olde Dartmouth territory. They were welcomed with open arms. Their emphasis on tolerance and egalitarianism attracted many residents of the area, and by the early 18th century were making a name for themselves all throughout the colony.

In Acushnet, the Quaker lifestyle had been adopted eagerly and was all the rage by the mid-18th century mark. Meetinghouses were being erected left and right in towns such as Rochester and New Bedford, but the residents of Acushnet wanted their own meetinghouse. In 1758, five Quakers by the names of John Sherman, Nehemiah Shearman, Daniel Wing, Nicholas Davis, and Russell Brayley, petitioned the Sandwich quarterly meeting, requesting permission to construct a meetinghouse. It was allowed with one stipulation: it must be built within the ensuing year.

The people of Acushnet responded with zeal, and the meetinghouse was up and running by June of 1759. In the next hundred years, Quakers rose to prominence, particularly as the heads of the whaling industry.

Nearly every whaling merchant or master of the time was a Quaker or had Quaker roots. In 1859, the Long Plain Meetinghouse was expanded in order to meet the growing demand of the Quaker community, and a carriage shed was built adjacent.

However, it was not long after this period of rapid growth and stigma that the Quakers started to lose relevance. Many people in Acushnet grew too affluent to respect the piety the Quaker life is predicated on, and thus converted to less ideologic denominations of Christianity, such as Unitarianism. By 1920, the Quaker congregation grew so small the meetinghouse was closed down due to lack of interest. It was briefly reopened a few years later, but was reclosed when the last of the Acushnet Quakers passed away in 1965. To the disappointment of the residents of Acushnet, the building which had once been a booming gathering place for religious devotees from all over the town quickly began to deteriorate. Due to pressure from active citizens, the Quakers drafted a proposal to sell the property to the Acushnet Historical Commission in 1985. The price? A single dollar. All the Historical Commission had to do was promise to restore and maintain the building while it was in their possession. The deal was quickly accepted.

The meetinghouse was fully restored and dedicated on October 12, 1991. State and foundation grants facilitated the process, and the Long Plain Meetinghouse was added to the National Register of Historical Places. It is one of only two buildings in all of Acushnet to boast this honor. Today, it is a vibrant public venue, holding concerts and socials frequently throughout the summer months.

HEAD OF THE RIVER

Known locally as River's End, the "Head of the River" district of Acushnet is one of the town's most iconic locations. It is Acushnet's very first historic district and, if it looks familiar, it may be because artists have been smitten by this quaint, picturesque area for centuries. One such artist was Clement Nye Swift, whose painting of the Head of the River bridge was so well received it was made the town's official seal. For many, that seal is what first comes to mind when the area is mentioned. Or maybe it is the beloved River's End Cafe. Or, more often than not, it is those dang, good-for-nothing, slow-as-molasses geese that somehow always manage to wait until I am fifteen minutes late to a meeting to waddle adorably into Main Street traffic and cause a twenty car back-up at the Tarkiln Hill Rd intersection. Or maybe that's just me. But I digress. What really should come to mind about the "Head of the River" is its esteemed place in the histories of both Acushnet and, on a larger scale, the United States of America. For starters, the River's End Cafe building was built in the year 1800 by William Rotch, making it over 200 years old. It served faithfully as the town's meat market for decades.

The bridge, however, is where United States history comes into play. Originally built with stone, today's bridge was built in 1959 to modernize the structure. However, certain parts of the first bridge are still visible. It was the original bridge that was once marched on by General Grey, a British commander who fought in the Revolution against the colonists. He had been ordered to burn houses and shops all over New Bedford, Fairhaven, and Acushnet to the ground. So in 1778, men from all over southeastern Massachusetts came to the Head of the River in Acushnet to face off against the Redcoats. The battle that ensued is referred to as both the "Engagement at the Bridge" and, because it is much cooler, the "Battle of the Bridge." The British were successfully vanquished that day, but not without a casualty. Lieut. Jonathan Metcalf, a fierce Colonial officer, lost his life and is said to be buried at the Acushnet Precinct Cemetery.

ACUSHNET-WESLEY UNITED METHODIST CHURCH

Okay, I'll admit it. I am a little biased on this one. Full disclosure, I was a member of the Acushnet-Wesley United Methodist Church for many years of my childhood, and just researching the building now has brought back many fond memories. However, you have no reason to be alarmed, as I have no need to personally sing the praises of this church. Its history not only as a cornerstone to Acushnet's centuries of progress, but as a testament to the willpower of its people, does that itself.

On August 7, 1807, history was made in the town of Acushnet. It was on this day that the first organized meeting of the Acushnet chapter of The First Methodist Episcopal Society took place in the loft of a man named William Kempton. Eight townspeople were baptized under his watch. One of the attendees, John Hawes, was so inspired by his baptism that he dedicated a portion of his property holdings to the Society in the hopes that one day a Methodist church might be built in the town of Acushnet. Little did Hawes know that his wish would come to fruition in only a matter of years, as his generous gift greatly expedited the process. Four years and $600 later, the First Methodist Episcopal Society Meeting House was built and dedicated. The building was unusually small and had no lathing, plastering, or painting. The church was really only held together by the will of its congregation. Footstoves were brought from people's homes for women and children to utilize, and bread on the Lord's Table was often frozen solid. Despite the church's many shortcomings, the structure stood standing and served the community for 42 years before being razed in 1853. In its place, a large white wooden church with a great spire was built that could better accommodate the growing congregation of the Methodist church. It was used for many years until tragedy struck on December 11, 1904. The wooden structure was burned to the ground in a presumed accident involving its coal heating system. This mishap shook the people of Acushnet as one of their most beloved and iconic buildings was lost seemingly for good.

However, the people of Acushnet have historically never been good at accepting defeat, particularly in the face of a conflagration. For the next year, people from all around the township came out to rebuild the church, lugging fieldstones from around their farms and homes with them, as well as a determination to regain what they all had lost. The result was a church that still stands today, proving that the tenacity of a community called upon to serve is a more reliable source of labor than any private, for-profit company ever could be.

The new stone church was dedicated on December 1, 1905. With it came a welcome new face for a congregation that had endured decades of struggle and disappointment: a priceless stained glass window depicting Jesus knocking on a door. The painting became the heart of the church, earning the acclaim of artists and fellow churchgoers alike all over the country. However, it appeared all was lost once again when on May 22, 1955 a fire broke out in the Sanctuary of the church. When firefighters came to put it out, it is said that Rev. John L. Dunham restrained them from chopping down the window. Luckily, the firefighters were still able to stop the fire before it spread and repairs to the sanctuary only took a few months. Thus, thanks to the reverend, the window still hangs in the building today, and can be seen illuminated at night for all who drive by the little stone church on Main Street.

WHELDEN MILL

Captain Joseph Whelden was a man of power. He had dedicated his life to the booming whaling industry and had worked his way up to the coveted captain rank. However, by the time he retired from the industry in the late 1700s, Whelden had already redirected his focus from sailing the high seas to what would eventually fill the gap whaling left in southeastern Massachusetts' commerce and labor: factorial production. Viva la Industrial Revolution.

Initially, Whelden purchased and maintained what was to be White's Cotton Factory. But following a very misguided hunch that the real money was a mile up the river, Whelden rid himself of his investment and built a larger cotton mill a short distance away in 1814. Assisting him in this project were Job Grey, Jr.; Loum Snow, Sr.; and the Swift boys, Jireh and Jonathan. They named their firm Whelden, Smith & Co. and, with all the blind ambition of men who cannot foresee their company's inevitable demise, set to work energetically. However, a few miles west, New Bedford found itself leaps and bounds ahead of Acushnet on the industrial spectrum; steam-powered mills were rendering measly water mills, such as the one owned by Captain Whelden, obsolete. So after a few years, the mill was put out of business. It was conveyed to the City of New Bedford in 1866 and has since deteriorated into ruin. However, out of the ashes of its predecessor, another cotton factory a mile away would emerge victorious.

WHITE'S COTTON FACTORY

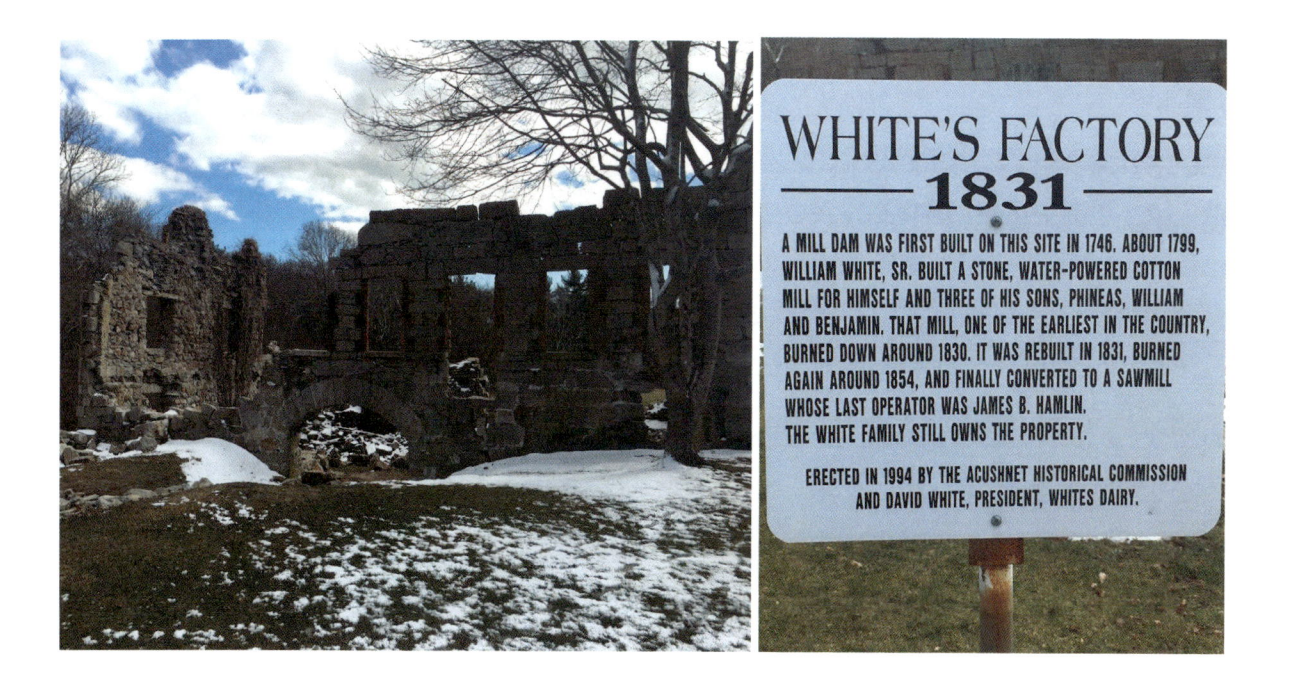

Hailed unanimously as the most photogenic location in Acushnet, White's Cotton Factory was once a bustling industrial site. Upon its purchase by William White, Sr. in 1799, an era of dynastic family influence began for the White's within the township of Acushnet. White and his three sons Phineas, William, and Benjamin took the site and turned it into a cotton mill servicing Fall River printworks. The factory was predicated on dying and working fulling cloth to be worn and used by residents all over eastern Massachusetts. However, what makes the building a true unsung treasure to the town of Acushnet is its historical antecedence in American industrialization; it was one of only a handful of cotton factories in the United States at the time of its establishment in 1799 (One other such cotton factory was operated famously under the control of our neighbors in Lowell). However, this landmark of Acushnet industry took a turn for the worst after burning down twice -- once in 1830 and again in around 1855. This was by no means a new occurrence for the town of Acushnet. Buildings burning down became the norm in that era due to lax attitudes towards fire safety initiatives. However, the former of the two fires prompted the White family to call it quits in 1844, and the factory and its surrounding lands became enthralled in a relentless buy-and-sell cycle that acted as a catalyst to its decay. The factory, scorched and exploited for all it was worth, slipped into a state of much-needed repair in the 1840's and then, soon after in the early 1900's, total dilapidation. Today, White's Cotton Factory not only stands proud as the backdrop to families wearing matching sweaters, but serves as a reminder of Acushnet's undeniable role as a leader of the Commonwealth during the era of American factorial production.

CAPTAIN FRANKLYN HOWLAND HOUSE

The Captain Franklyn Howland house was built around 1844 as the "Union Seminary." It was a boarding school that was nearly twice the size it is now. When the Union Seminary was decidedly taking up more space than it was worth, it was split into two parts. One part stayed where it was and became the Howland household, while the other was moved across the street and purchased by a man named Samuel Cory.

It is important that Captain Franklyn Howland is given special acknowledgement at this point in my writing. Without him, the history of Acushnet would be much murkier than it is today, and this historical account would be nearly impossible to write.

Howland was born in Little Compton, RI. By the time he turned 16, Howland had already been exposed to the work force at an importing house at New York City. He worked there until the outbreak of the Civil War in 1861, when he enrolled without hesitation to fight for the preservation of the Union. He was 18 years old. However, amidst the heat of battle, Howland was captured by Confederate forces and suffered as a prisoner of war for over a year. Due to mistreatment, Howland paralyzed his spine and lost almost all ability to maneuver his body. This would have stopped a lesser man, but not Captain Franklyn Howland. He went on to serve as a United States pension attorney, justice of the peace, and probate attorney for about 30 years after the war. Most notably, in regards to the history of Acushnet, Howland also served as the town historian. During his time in this position, Howland wrote the book *A History of the Town of Acushnet*. He passed away, however, before he could complete it in 1907. It was published posthumously, and can be purchased to this day at the Long Plain Museum. If you have enjoyed reading about the history of Acushnet thus far (which I am sure you did!), I highly recommend picking up a copy. This has only been the tip of the iceberg, and if you are interested in learning about Acushnet's role in the smallpox epidemic, the Revolutionary War, or even slavery, then Howland's piece is a must-read.

MILESTONE 9

Around the year 1850, the town of Fairhaven initiated a new system meant to facilitate navigation within the town. Granite stones were placed along a route that led from the center of Fairhaven to the outskirts of Rochester in an effort for residents to more efficiently orient their location. At each given mile along the route, a stone was erected inscribed "FH" for Fairhaven along with a number indicating how many miles the stone was from the town hall. In those times, Acushnet was a subdivision of the town of Fairhaven. For this reason, many of the stones that were erected in those times are still standing in Acushnet today. Only five remain total, and ones such as Milestone 8 above have clearly weathered the sands of time. Milestones 6, 7, and 8 can be seen along Main Street, whereas "Milestone 9" lies farthest North along the Rochester town line.

PERRY HILL CHURCH

Another keepsake from Acushnet's time as northern Fairhaven is the Perry Hill Church. It is a direct successor of the First Christian Society of North Fairhaven. The church is a town rarity; it stands as the only remaining Greek Revival Church building in Acushnet.

The origins of the Perry Hill Church are a bit complicated. The original owners of the land prior to the construction of the church were John Perry and Albert Allen. They then sold the land to George Mandell. It was shortly after the sale had been completed, however, that Perry, Allen, Ansel White, and assorted trustees of The First Christian Society of North Fairhaven decided Fairhaven needed another church -- and it had to be on that plot of land they had just sold. With a little luck and persuasion (and $1500 in cash) Mandell agreed to give them back their land. That $1500 is the equivalent of $43,124 today, so for no real stake in this little plot of land, it is safe to say Mandell was more than satisfied with the turn of events.

It took a few years, but in 1851 the Perry Hill Church was completed and dedicated. The first active members of the church were John Perry, Lemual Perry, John Blackmer, William Gammons, Joseph Taber, William Jenne, Betsy M. Coin, Bibel White, Jane Cathell, Rebecca Taber, Amy

Cook, Abigail Gammons, Patience Cory, and Lois Blackmer. It took less than a year for this congregation to find a minister. His name was William D. Haley; he was ordained at the church within the same year it was built. Since its construction in 1851, the church kept few to no records. The only records prior to 1883 were ones written in 1867, extending the right of franchise on all church matters to women of the congregation. While this may be the only record kept, it is also one of utmost importance. It reflects Acushnet's progressive action regarding women's rights in a time when gender equality was a mere afterthought, as well as the role of the church in such a controversial matter. Today, a local Boy Scout from Acushnet is doing his part to preserve the town's rich history. Logan Avelar is restoring the Perry Hill Church building for his Eagle project. The renovation entails repainting the entire floor as well as all the church pews.

LEONARD BOAT SHOP

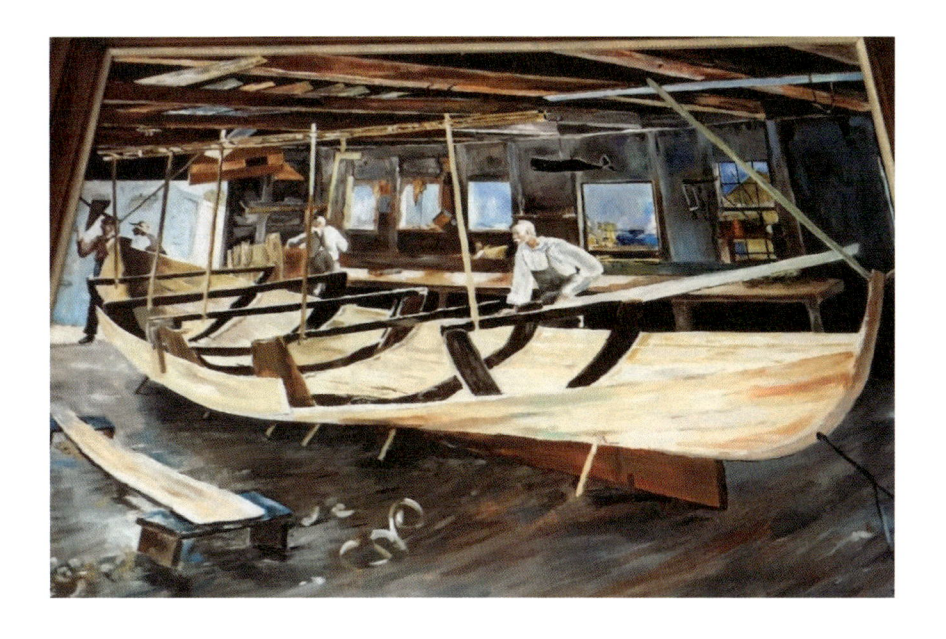

I feel it would be remiss if somewhere in this history of Acushnet I did not mention whaling. After all, coastal Massachusetts from around 1823, when New Bedford overpowered Nantucket as the country's premier whaling city, until 1886, when it lost that title to San Francisco, was famous for its pull in the whaling industry. However, what often goes overlooked is the role of Acushnet in the affair. Outside of the manpower it contributed, it also dipped its toes into naval construction, or shipbuilding. The most salient example of this contribution is the Leonard Boat Shop, located fittingly on Leonard Street. This ma-and-pa shop was originally owned by Thomas Severance, who sold it off after the Revolutionary War. It was then tossed around like a hot potato between a number of ambitious upstart entrepreneurs until around 1852, when one of those entrepreneurs slipped a glove on, caught that hot potato, and turned it into a shipbuilding workhouse. This man was Ebenezer Leonard, who worked relentlessly building an inordinate amount of ships for decades after his purchase. Fortunately, he was able to turn that hard work into fat stacks of money due to the hungry supply-and-demand of the whaling era sweetspot: the 1850's to the 1870's.

Leonard's involvement in this profitable enterprise continued on until his death in 1891, when his two sons, Eben and Charles, took over the family business. Together, they took the Leonard Boat Shop up a notch, producing over 1,000 whaling boats in a 25 year span. They became world famous; their ambition was not restrained to the New Bedford area solely. The Leonard boats were held in high regard all over the country, and were docked all throughout American coastline. However, in 1916, the Leonard brothers ceased production and shut the doors of the Leonard Boat Shop. This was most likely due to New Bedford's slipping grasp on the whaling industry and pressure from environmental reformers. However, what the Leonard family was able to accomplish in their time has, and will, live on as a key component of Acushnet's whaling legacy. The painting above was done by Cynthia Leonard.

LAURA KEENE FARMHOUSE

For a small town landmark to have ties to one famous person in history is a rarity in and of itself; for it to have ties to *two* famous people in history is unheard of. However, thus is the case with the Laura Keene farmhouse, today located at 59 South Main Street. It was originally known as the Kempton Farm until it was purchased by British stage actress and theater manager Laura Keene in 1865. The original home was burned down in 1897 and rebuilt in 1899 as it stands today.

William Bradford was a romanticist painter out of New Bedford whose love for his art was matched only by his love for his community. Bradford's favorite subject to paint was the New Bedford harbor, specifically the ships. His love for the southcoast began in 1823, when Bradford was born in the little Kempton farmhouse on South Main Street. To this day, Bradford is considered the most renowned artist to have roots in the Acushnet/Fairhaven area.

As my keen readers have probably already deduced, Laura Keene is the other famous person aforementioned. While Laura Keene may not have been born in Acushnet, her love for the area proved on par with that of Bradford. She was born in the United Kingdom on July 20, 1826 as Mary Frances Moss. Keene changed her name after her husband, Henry Wellington Taylor, was convicted of a crime and sent to an Australian penal colony. When Keene travelled to Australia to officiate their divorce years later, she claimed to have never found him. Some believe she found him but, upon demanding the divorce, he refused. Regardless, Keene and her husband were technically married til death did them part in 1860 when Taylor passed away. However, Keene had bigger things on her plate than a fake marriage. She dreamed of becoming an actress. This dream became a fruitful career for Keene as she rose to stardom in the United States. She went on to purchase her very own American theater where she found success in both theater management and acting. By April 14, 1865, Keene had established herself as an accomplished actress, and was starring in the play *Our American Cousin* at Ford's Theater in Washington, DC. In the middle of her performance, however, President Abraham Lincoln was shot and killed by John Wilkes Booth. Keene was one of the last people to comfort the president prior to his passing at the theater. As she was cradling the dying president, some blood from Lincoln's wound stained the cuff of her dress. The cuff can be seen in the National Museum of American History today.

    Following this traumatic experience, Keene sought the comfort of a simple life, and what better place to find refuge from the harsh realities of everyday life than the town of Acushnet? Keene relocated her and her children parttime to 59 South Main Street in 1865, immediately after Lincoln's assassination. By 1869, Keene was ready to return to world of theater. She served as the manager of Chestnut Theater in Philadelphia where she owned a second home before passing away in Montclair, New Jersey in 1873 due to tuberculosis. She was only 47 years old.

PARTING WAYS SCHOOLHOUSE

I am a proud Blue Devil. I am also a bit of a company man. Which is why, as I combed through my research in the early stages of this project, I was pleasantly surprised to find none other than Henry Huttleston Rogers's portrait staring up at me beside a picture of the Parting Ways Schoolhouse.

For the uninformed, Henry Huttleston Rogers was a tycoon of the oil industry in the mid to late 1800s. He was born in Mattapoisett but spent much of his childhood in the Fairhaven area. His work in the Standard Oil company brought him wealth that rivaled even the Rockefellers, his compatriots in the oil industry. Much of this fortune was given back to his hometown in the form of building funds, most notably being my own Fairhaven High School, as well as the Millicent Library. However, what very few know is Huttleston Rogers's contribution to the town of Acushnet. Built one year prior to the Long Plain Schoolhouse was the Parting Ways Schoolhouse. It was Acushnet's very first graded school and, as a result, helped push Acushnet into the fold of enlightened public education that was sweeping the country at the time of its inception in 1874. However, in 1903, it was decided the schoolhouse was too small to accommodate the large number of students enrolled. The solution: a grant from Henry Huttleston Rogers himself. It was enlarged to four rooms, resembling the building that can be seen today.

At the time of this writing, what was the Parting Ways Schoolhouse is today the Police and Health Departments. However, the Acushnet Police Department is currently taking up new residency on Middle Road in the form of a $5.2 million police station that was approved by voters in 2012. Although Acushnet's finest surely appreciate the historical relevance of their station, the building is simply too outdated for the policemen of the 21st century, as they are well overdue for a more modern station.

LONG PLAIN SCHOOL

School House Long Plain.

If it weren't for this building right here, this book would not have been possible. What was the Long Plain Schoolhouse is today the Long Plain Museum, your go-to for any know-how needed on the history of Acushnet. I've spent a lot of time here, conducting research and taking in its abundance of information, and it is in my own informed opinion that nowhere else in the town of Acushnet can you feel as historically anchored to the community as you are when you are standing in this building. If you have not checked it out, I highly recommend it, as it is an experience that you cannot get anywhere else.

The Long Plain Schoolhouse was started in 1875 at the hands of Rebecca H. Davis, with help from her parents Humphrey and Eunice. The family was very well respected; they were renowned for their charisma and benevolence. For a little historical context, the great Horace Mann had already begun his crusade on public education at the time of this school's establishment in 1875; however, Mann's ideals had not yet been enforced universally, as public schools of this era were still synonymous with being cruel, unsanitary, and underfunded. So when word got out that the kind, trustworthy Davis's were starting up a school for children, families from all over southeastern Massachusetts rushed to get their kids on the roster. It was enjoyed and utilized as a school for decades, until it was closed in

1972 and reopened as the history museum it is today. The Long Plain School was listed July 17, 2012 on the National Register of Historic Places.

Historical landmarks are interesting in and of themselves, but those with fun side stories, such as the Long Plain Schoolhouse, are even more interesting. The year was 1838 when Reverend Ira Leland took up teaching at the Long Plain Schoolhouse. Beloved by the community, Leland settled comfortably into his role as a leader in the township. He was energetic, well-educated, and young, three vital characteristics when it comes to educating youth. These traits also caught the eye of his employer, Rebecca Davis, and at the risk of being the subject of town gossip, the two were married shortly after his hiring and lived together happily for years to come. This romantic anecdote just goes to show that history does not have to be boring -- in fact it never truly is, so long as one is willing to dig a little deeper in the record books.

RUSSELL MEMORIAL LIBRARY

Today we live in a culture plagued by a universal lack of appreciation for what once was revolutionary. In an age of technological discovery, this applies to a number of things that the general public has come to see as "obsolete", but for the purpose of this writing I am going to narrow the scope down to libraries. I believe that the fast and efficient access to information that predicates our electronic world actually augments, not diminishes, the necessity for local libraries. In this hectic, mile-a-minute society, a place to quietly sit, read, or just think without the distractions of the outside world has never been more vital. This is what I imagine Captain George Parker, Anna Bradford, and Emily Brownell had in mind when they established the Russell Memorial Library on June 13, 1896, a mere 36 years after the town's incorporation. It was the first library in Acushnet, and had only $100 to its name when it first started out. Each year the government would donate $100 to the library in order for it to build up its book collection. However, once the town began to utilize and cherish the library, the government upped that amount to $150 annually. The library's success also led to the establishment of two other branch libraries in Acushnet: one at Long Plain and one at Perry Hill. It was named in honor of George and Ruby Russell, the former being a beloved educator within the township.

In recent news, the Russell Memorial Library was closed on December 5, 2015. The building had become too weathered as a result of being the town's library for over a century. It also lacked sufficient handicap accessibility. The library was relocated to the Howard School building and the Board of Selectmen will decide what is to become of the old Russell Memorial Library.

RICHARD DAVIS VARIETY STORE

Born in 1847, a man by the name of Richard Davis, Jr. came to adulthood during the Civil War era. In those years, when it came time for a family to restock on supplies for their homes, Mom could not print out some online coupons, load up the kids in the Toyota minivan, and peruse the shelves of Walmart. But what Mom could do was count up her paper notes, pile the kids into a horse-drawn buggie, and make a beeline for Richard Davis's Variety Store.

Richard Davis, Jr. was Acushnet's first genuine Renaissance man. He served as the official postmaster of the Long Plain Village, superintendent of the Long Plain Meeting House, and the proud owner of the business his father, Richard Davis, Sr., started in 1885. The Variety Store was both popular and profitable, making a name for itself as the go-to stop for everyday goods. Which it was, until it was burned down in 1883 due to a dropped lantern. This was by no means a new occurrence for the town of Acushnet. Buildings burning down became the norm in that era due to lax attitudes towards fire safety initiatives. But what was unexpected about the burning of the Variety Store was Richard Davis, Jr.'s ambitious response. Davis rebuilt the store from the ground up on the opposite side of Main Street, where the structure still stands to this day.

Acknowledgments

At this point, I would like to pay homage to the many people who contributed to this book. This was in no way a one-person job; this book was completed at the hands of an entire community. Specifically, I would like to thank the Acushnet Historical Society. I was welcomed with open arms into this vibrant organization, and was assisted every step of the way by their president, Pauline Teixeira, and every member involved. Next, I would like to thank my Boy Scout troop. Troop 51 did more than just guide me through this rigorous course to my Eagle. Troop 51 helped make me into the man I am today. Without their support, I would never have had the ability to achieve the coveted Eagle Scout rank. Finally, I would like to thank my parents. They have made many sacrifices to get me to the point I am today, and they will never know how much I appreciate them for it.

And thank you, my kind reader. I hope you enjoyed learning about the history of Acushnet as much as I did. The citizens of this town are incredibly fortunate to live in a community so rich in history, and I believe many take this for granted simply because they are unaware. This was my motivation in writing this book; I hope that the people who read this take away from it a greater sense of appreciation for the town and its history. I know this book has augmented by love for this community, and I am proud to have grown up in a "peaceful resting place near water." Thank you.

Made in the USA
Charleston, SC
29 August 2016